HERE, THERE, AND WHAT IS BROKEN IN BETWEEN

NNEOMA VERONICA NWOGU

This is a work of fiction. All names, characters, places, and incidents are a product of the author's imagination. Any resemblance to real events or persons, living or dead, is entirely coincidental.

Published by Akashic Books
©2023 Nneoma Veronica Nwogu
ISBN: 978-1-63614-125-1

All rights reserved
Printed in China
First printing

Akashic Books
Brooklyn, New York
Instagram, Twitter, Facebook: @AkashicBooks
E-mail: info@akashicbooks.com
Website: www.akashicbooks.com

African Poetry Book Fund
Prairie Schooner
University of Nebraska
110 Andrews Hall
Lincoln, Nebraska 68588

TABLE OF CONTENTS

Preface by Saddiq Dzukogi 5

"Ebo Landing" warrior 9
On Pa's grave 14
Naija 15
Memories 17
Red eye 18
At the warden's drinks 19
In the room (at the table) 21
A rare evening in late July 24
Responsorial dirge 26
Exiles? 29
If I wrote about yam 31
Hearth-coming 36

Acknowledgments 38

PREFACE
by Saddiq Dzukogi

Nneoma Veronica Nwogu has delicately crafted a world where past and present are engrossed in a visceral rapport that explores spaces of spiritual and mundane existences. Here she exults, in joy and praise songs, those spaces of intimacy and vulnerability with clear and poignant lyrical insight. Reading through this chapbook feels, in part, like an act of worship, a celebration of ancestral ties that refuses the blunt of time and the rupture of migration, colonization, and exile.

> The dust rose to envelop and blind us
> and where we would stomp down the rains
> to slay the dust, the night broke loose
> from the Iroko and cast us like trapped hyenas
> into the netherworld where the sea people
> roasted our children between endless skies
> eating their brains with pitch forks and liquor
> while we, harnessed to giant boats, floated
> in the swamp of our excrement and drowned
> the earth-quaking wailings of our violated daughters.

("'Ebo Landing' warrior")

Nwogu confronts slavery in a composite narrative that takes responsibility and centers the experience of enslaved Africans from an African perspective, subverting the notion of the civility of the "sea people" who "roasted . . . children between endless skies / eating their brains with pitch forks and liquor" ("'Ebo Landing' warrior"). So brutal was the treatment that even "the day [and] night" as they "frolicked" were apportioned blame for the crime of witness. Nwogu, when she writes "The gods had been slaughtered, I was certain," in a way strips deities of their divination for abandoning "a kinsman [who] has been whipped / again . . . hanging upside down / from a pole . . ." This is Nwogu's way of pointing a finger at the "gods," a suggestive gesture that points to ancestral African complicity in the enslavement of other Africans. Here Africa's scar of complicity is bare for all to see:

> "*Osimmiri duru anyi bia,*
> *Osimmiri duru anyi laa*"
> The faces of my clansmen depict my thoughts.
> In silence we nod, our *chi* had come along.
> It was time to fight, to release our souls
> and take back the spirit of Igbo land
> "Deep waters, you led us here
> Deep waters now lead us home."
> "Deep waters, you led us here
> Deep waters now lead us home."
>
> ("'Ebo Landing' warrior")

In a work of spirituality imbued with the cadence of celebration and prayer, Nwogu pays homage to ancestors, "elders," and the tradition they have cultivated, a tradition which is the preoccupation of her poetic drift and which she excavates. Through poesy of immense aural brilliance, Nwogu reenacts the sophisticated social system of the Igbo people, their music, their valor, and their religion "to the accompaniment" of her own contemporary sounds and instincts that seek to preserve for herself these rich customs, threatened, perhaps, by modernity and her own state of "exile." With impeccable attention and incantatory wit, Nwogu, "as she stares at the weeping clouds," hears even the "squabble" of "gods," "elders," and ancestors centering her own view of history ("On Pa's grave").

Here, there, and what is broken in between is a world where the celestial is explicated with ease and beauty. There is ritual, in these verses, of the communion between the ordinary and the extraordinary, between land, gods, and humans—a ritual inclusive of the clan-folks stolen for the land across the sea. There is mythmaking here, a careful building of a world of endless intrigue, where "the day frolicked with the night, each chasing / the other, laughing . . ." ("'Ebo Landing' warrior").

What I find most striking about this chapbook is its attention to small things that seem unremarkable until they become the subject of our desires. She reminds us that because of the sudden distance created by leaving home, a constant state of comparison emerges. Soon, most things encountered while away from home tend to lead us back home.

The community that Nwogu extends is cosmic, one that not even death can break:

> as huts puff out smoke
> declaring the clan's evening mealtime
> and soon she will have to join.
>
> For now, she lies by Pa
> and tells the tale of the day
> savoring the precious time
>
> ("On Pa's grave")

In expressing the anxiety of multiple identities, begotten from the violence of colonization and slavery, and of global belonging, Nwogu laments being torn between "the home I have always known / to the hearth of your younger years / Pa . . ." ("Exiles?").

In Nwogu's sensory-rich poems, she shows herself to be a poet of immense range, writing richly about the communal with such personal vision that blossoms even more when she writes about grief with a palpable intimacy:

> As I, your child, libate the earth
> pleading for you a good return,
> I also pray in a foreign tongue
> your spirit chose to miss the plane.
>
> If indeed you are here watching
> my faulty steps dance the *Ese,*
> you must see why I will forbid
> posterity to bring me here.
>
> Born in exile, have I become
> a guest in my ancestral hearth;
> displaced, my spirit wanders here
> and finds its rest when cast away.
>
> Pa, I take this past you have craved
> for so long and leave it to you.
>
> ("Exiles?")

This is a poet whose work will continue to sing with a voice that will become even clearer, more beautiful, and plangent.

"EBO LANDING" WARRIOR
To the accompaniment of Igbo flute and drum

I

The sweet smell of palm wine
drifted through the homestead
to drench the dry but rooted bones
of sleeping elders as pregnant gourds,
hung high in the trees, awaited
the tapping pleas of intercessors,
and bided their time to libate the land.
In the obi, a cutlass submitted
to my kinsman's sharpening stone
with hopes for an early foray to the forest
where hunters murmur hurried greetings
in reply to the laughter of maidens
on the footpath, heeding only
the groans of unlucky hyenas.
The sound of morning rising
urged wrapper-clad women to the stream
fretting babies lodged safely on their backs
as the clan's gong called from faraway
summoning councils to solve disputes,
when I washed the kindred's worried feet
and placed them on the road to the *Aro* priest.

The moon, full, having appeased the big *Afo*
for its fourth coming, headed home
unsure of what mood the sun will wake
leaving the Iroko, in their matrimonial ritual,
to gather in the shadows, the spirits

and hold the night for the day.
Just behind the moon, I marched steadily
holding in my sack two white pigeons
and a pound of river clay.
The gods had summoned the warriors of the clans
in the face of dissenting elders and ancestors
to carry a disquieting peace to the sea people
to whom the land was neither mortal nor sacred
and we, weighing our strength, obeyed the gods,
for the seasons had settled into a pandemonium
stealing unripe men and maidens for the sea.

At the four crossroads of our clans
we gathered, all eight, to wait
for the priest while the young ones
encircled us to chant the warrior's songs.

Nzogbu! Nzogbu! Enyi mba!
Zogbue nwoke, Enyi mba, Zogbuo nwanyi—
knowing our mission, we forcefully
feigned to trample the foreign elephant.

II

The dust rose to envelop and blind us
and where we would stomp down the rains
to slay the dust, the night broke loose
from the Iroko and cast us like trapped hyenas
into the netherworld where the sea people
roasted our children between endless skies
eating their brains with pitch forks and liquor
while we, harnessed to giant boats, floated

in the swamp of our excrement and drowned
the earth-quaking wailings of our violated daughters.
The day frolicked with the night, each chasing
the other, laughing with the sea people
as they bound the weak ones to large rocks
and sent them on a futile errand
to crack the ocean's bottom.

The gods had been slaughtered,
I was certain.
We were so far from the land
and yet nowhere near the ancestral world.
Now, I wake to the warning
shrieks of crickets and birds
I do not recognize.
A kinsman has been whipped
again.
He is silent,
hanging upside down
from a pole and we are near
the land—
a land.
Holding my valor, I struggle
to stand and stop
the trembling veins, the chattering teeth.
Around me, warriors breath in fear,
scrounging for refuge in living corpses.
Chained hands cover what is
now the sign of our defeat,
knowing we are
no longer warriors,

nor the living,
nor the dead.

They lead us in chains
from the edge of the sea
plodding through
a thin and miserable swamp,
toward their forest, flooded with palms.
A kinswoman stumbles
against crushed grass.
She is whipped
and I wait,
looking to the heavens.
The palms look diseased unlike the ones at home.
The sky is lit but the sun is lost.
The air is burdened
with tears and now
it dawns—
this forest has been visited.
Amadioha has been here.

I notice a shadow in a stagnant pool
and I long to follow or just to stoop
and quench my thirst but the chains
on my feet are clogged with mud.
The blood of my kinsman trickles into the pool
a sharp twig pierced his worn-out heel.
I look at him and a spirit dashes across
and then, two, then three and more
and more . . .

From the wind, the chant comes
bearing the anger of our gods,
our children, our spirits
our maidens and ancestors
our mothers and elders
in the roar of fearless warriors.

III

"*Osimmiri duru anyi bia*
Osimmiri duru anyi laa."
The faces of my clansmen depict my thoughts.
In silence we nod, our *chi* had come along.
It was time to fight, to release our souls
and take back the spirit of Igbo land
"Deep waters, you led us here
Deep waters now lead us home."
"Deep waters, you led us here
Deep waters now lead us home."

IV

As we walk backwards with our song
amidst the tawai! of their whips
their faces cloud up
with fear and despair
as they watch us
drag death
by its ear
to the sea.

ON PA'S GRAVE

The hostile rain of the monsoon season
causes the thunder gods to squabble
and send their warning flashes zipping
across the dark September sky.

She lies on the paved mound
and listens to the painful pelts
on the poor aluminum top
held by four pillar posts.

Her head lies on her palms,
her caked feet bare, her ankles crossed
as she stares at the weeping clouds.

The compound has been silenced
as huts puff out smoke
declaring the clan's evening mealtime
and soon she will have to join.

For now, she lies by Pa
and tells the tale of the day
savoring the precious time
that is Pa's and hers alone.

NAIJA

They shake hands.
Smiling, he envelops
that hand in his two hands,
nodding vigorously
as soon as
that head was dipped.
They turn to us.
They wave.
They look at each other
and they turn again
and they wave . . . and wave.
His teeth were gleaming
in the sun
almost a laugh.
The other easily smiled,
his skin, a shiny mahogany,
the other, ivory lightly burned.

The talking drums
respond
to the rhythmic vicious slaps
of familiar hands,
as we sing and dance.
The masquerades glide
royally across the arena.
The sound of the gong
vibrates
clearly in answer
to the pumping heart of the crowd,

the call, an echo
Zik! ... *trick*
Awo! ... *wayo*
Zik! ... *trick*
Awo! ... *wayo*

It was Independence.

MEMORIES

the lid of an immigrant box
slowly shuts
on the eve of the long journey
ignoring the hands behind
splayed
over a weary faced clock:
a loaded dawn

RED EYE

Suspended there in deep blue dreams
amidst the dust in a golden sky
nursing the chronic blink of beams
without a care like a broken eye
it slices through the stream of winds
strutting its un-flapping wings.

AT THE WARDEN'S DRINKS

With an outstretched hand
he parted the air
and puffing peach filled cheeks
in Queen's English
he'd said,

"And you are . . . ?"

chuckle—"Who am I?"—chuckle
one, slight
cough, clear throat

"Nigerian by colonization
but Igbo by extraction
made American by citizenship
grew bohemian in aesthetics
partly British in scholarship
wholly global in politics."

a raised brow, an aborted smirk

"Do you mean my class?
oh, at once crème de la crème
and bottom of the barrel
drinking tea over Lewis
and Berkeley,
yet serving,
not too rare,
bits of history

to those for whom
the sight of me is education."

His weapon retreats
without a wave,
his nerves stagger—
a negotiated peace
settles
when I smile
and sidestep to
pause
a bloodless war.

IN THE ROOM (AT THE TABLE)

just then, arms fall
and shoulders reach
for the ground, their blades
inch slowly apart
trembling
three fingers huddle
a trinity, reluctant
to bear the pen

words tumble over words
for far-flung worlds, fiats
promoting poverty
elimination

in fabricated nations, communities
imagine
heads protruding
from rounded bellies
belching starvation
and dancing for mercy
aid for death
or salvation

we scramble: eight men,
two women, scions
of conquerors
and I
to make up

the solution
we decide

is it guiltless
if Judas, without
a choice
sealed the fate
of the condemned
in search of peace?

white thin walls draw lines
expanding the universe
multiplying numbers
of people dividing
happiness subtracting
children, to create
a dream

is the table the fruit
ripened from roots
that invaded the land
unrestrained?

without a choice,
I sell a continent,
dense with its promise
filling the silent room
with the excess—
remnants of pain and pride,
a patois of faith
reason and fury
on behalf of, for the benefit of, in consideration of

I speak

for a minute and a breath
followed with paced continuance
as though, I had been a pause, a moment of silence
in which nothing happened and
dying nations died.

twenty minutes into this decision
meeting, the silver
weighs heaviest and in this hour
I live eternity
in hades.

A RARE EVENING IN LATE JULY

The sun sails the river
setting for Virginia
in rays as gold
soaks the aging
leaves hanging on
trees in the backyards
of Kalorama Road.
Behind trails the trifling
air—an estranged cousin
to the well-known wave
familiar to absent politicians.
The orange clouds are still.

Across the narrow alley
in gray shorts and white tee,
a man flips a burger
and slowly shuts the grill.
The French poodle upstairs is barking
for a decent walk around the park.
Here, on the balcony,
the fragrance of jasmines
mates with the Duke of Cambridge
and the purple queen peers
over the white railings, ignoring
the solicitations of ferns and lemongrass.
The scraping of a patio
next door gradually dims
to the birds humming
along to a country

song on the radio.
Lights stroll in
one after another
on the bridge, streak-free
through windows of family
rooms living in old-century homes.
The sky sits back in pale blue
grateful for the time
taking in the view.

RESPONSORIAL DIRGE

...like your mother's hair
reflects the sun
in reddish hue,
my skin glows
and is as brown.

tell them

...my smile unsealed a trail
where the color of blood ran
blind on winter nights,
and we hand in hand, unafraid,
knocked door to door
anxious to midwife
our kind of America.

tell them

...my nibbles, inky in edges
you craved, charged "enslaving"
has etched
a life illumined,
as a lantern in a forest night,
by love
alone
all over you.

tell them

... our love danced naked
to the melody of city skylights at night,
the soft spectrum of blue-red reflections
on high-rises
Sisyphean sirens, the sound of life losing,
calling us to arms, willing us to live.
yes, yes, yes!

tell them

... it waltzed in and out of kaleidoscopes
anticipating a beautiful dawn,
amidst hot coals erupting
from the horizon of a calm ocean.

tell them

... it was the sun swimming ashore
in pursuit of smooth, grainy then smooth
lavender waves—enfolding.

tell them

... in my darkness, drowning
you yelled,
a skip short of perfect beat
"you tell me / what the fuck / I tell my folks?"

tell them

. . . like the bush of perky green pudica
that caress the outer compounds
of my childhood, waded through
by careless hands and witless feet.

tell them
wordlessly, I died.

EXILES?

From the home I have always known
to the hearth of your younger years,
Pa, I've brought you.

The warriors of David are now
vultures prowling to eat your flesh
and that tree's fruit cannot be told,
Pa, from those of fading flowers.

Their eyes seem to mourn you with me
but that glare at my well-worn bags
tell their loss is not you but things
I have not brought from where I come.

As I, your child, libate the earth
pleading for you a good return,
I also pray in a foreign tongue
your spirit chose to miss the plane.

If indeed you are here watching
my faulty steps dance the *Ese,*
you must see why I will forbid
posterity to bring me here.

Born in exile, have I become
a guest in my ancestral hearth;
displaced, my spirit wanders here
and finds its rest when cast away.

Pa, I take this past you have craved
for so long and leave it to you.

IF I WROTE ABOUT YAM

In simple words,
just boil
with salt
and serve
with oil.
If I tell you
of the many ways,
roasted or fried
potage or steamed
pounded or grilled,
yam is
the symbol for Igbo.
Alpha-beta of a tongue,
in the sacred text
the other half of power.
Oh, to hold the knife
and the yam!

In the beginning 'twas a word
seeming like "I am"
but now, is the road
to the old days with my father
between the city I'd called home
and the teeming ancestral town.
It is the feast and the place.
Iri Ji
—the new yam festival.
If you read closely
—the yam eating festival.

In essence, the harvest
and in that particular town
we called it
Ji-Mbaise.
Mbaise being the town
it meant Mbaise yam
because it was not just any yam,
it was *Ji-Mbaise.*
The sound of the phrase
demanded a full mouth
bursting like lit gun powder.
It felt rooted and strong,
in our Catholic home
August 15
is a feast day
only known as
Ji-Mbaise.

Yam is the night split wide open
spilling the daylight out
of foreign-made generators
forcing the dense darkness of the rain forest
to draw back, enfolding in itself
the soul-force of kinsfolk
carried in the chatter
of twilight creatures, drums booming
at the retreat and all
that is left of the dead
is silence.
As elders gather in greeting
Igbo Kwenu! Kwenu! Kwezuenu!

fists crossing fists at the wrists
titled canes gently touching, head to head
and bare-chested men wrestle at the square
muscles dancing for young women watching
while wives and mothers of husbands cook
and feed and sing and revel in the feast.
Ji-Mbaise.

It is the village children playing
with their city cousins in compounds,
in the market place, where they mimic
the masquerades who, out of nowhere
break off into sprints, chasing the children—
who dare come out
to watch them
and follow them—
then stop
to dance for a frightened child
who'd sought the crook of safe kindred hands.
This towering pyramid of layered raffia skirt and oversized mask
the enormity of their size in movement, now a marvel.
Ji-Mbaise.

It is the palm wine and Stout
Guinness and Star
even Fanta and Coke
but also in the shadows,
the *Kai-Kai* in tin cans
in pursuit of the yam,
roasted and served with red palm oil,
steamed in light but spicy fish soups,

concocted in *ngwongwo*, a kind of gumbo
and for the frail fairies from the city,
plain fried with egg sauce. [there is
always something
for the madness in all of us.]
Ji-Mbaise

It is teenage boys stealing
tube-shaped types
jostling to roast them over open fires
for the winner of the name duel,
and then twisting pointed knives through the tube,
to fill the hole with ground hot *ose*
If I call you and you answer, you lose.
If you call me, and I tell you
"You call and you answer," I win.
And you roast in the courtyards
within the brick front house and clay kitchen line
where spaces are swept clean for combat.
Battling boys gather to see
who can consume a smoking hot tube
with an unflinching gaze and fiery tongue.
Cough or let a speck fall
on that hallowed ground
you lose to *chei*!
groans and pledge
to roast another day
besieged with thoughts
of when to steal and how to stuff
the yam to cut a boy
to earth or down a size.

A trojan horse!
Ji-Mbaise.

It is the libation
to earth—god of harvest, giver of the yam
to those just beyond
ensconced in the crowd,
that spirit-human vibration.
Igbo-ness, which formed
like a bone inside me,
creating at once solidity and tenderness—
this steadfast trunk
bearing the branches
of my multiplicity.

HEARTH-COMING

Shine-shine!
The clouds spread
over the Sahara,
a fistful of farina powder
in boiling water,
steamy red
terrains running
from the Kalahari,
the aftermath of a tryst
between a sweaty sun and his fertile earth.
Flowers whistle
hawking their goods along
the routes of Kirstenbosch,
harmattan purples,
tongue-ish pinks,
dusty orange, and curry yellows
like "cash and carry" in Onitsha main market, cheering
as toddler clouds cuddle
the nooks of Kilimanjaro,
then free fall from the edge
of the Table,
head first
into the belly of the Niger
catcalling to copy the Thundering Smoke.

The smoke of rain?
No, goat meat roasting,
palm oil frying ripe dodo and fish.
The rain of sound?

Yes,
fresh fufu pounding,
oil bean seeds
popping,
tingling tips of dark fingers
on a bamboo flute.
Two jeje sticks skip-hop-skipping
on an indulgent xylophone
teasing the ear like a shy sneeze
that grabs onto nose hairs,
too afraid to see the world.

Iya! the African child is finally home!

ACKNOWLEDGMENTS

"'Ebo Landing' warrior" is inspired by Carrie Mae Weems's *Ebo Landing* photograph.

"Exiles?" responds to Abena Busia's poem "Exiles" and pays homage to David Diop's poem "Africa." *Ese* is an Igbo burial dance.